"Mark Paulson h
creatively uses the
cant Biblical princ
beautifully illust:
God and with our brothers and
the amazing potential to change lives and to bring all of us
closer to the Lord." —**Patrick Kavanaugh,** Executive Director
Christian Performing Artists' Fellowship
Artistic Director, The MasterWorks Festival
Dean, Grace College School of Music

"Christian musicians face a constant battle balancing musical excellence, and the worldly accolades it brings, with Christian commitment, and the Christ-like humility it requires. In *God's Cycle of Music* Mark Paulson uses music-based metaphors and analogies to clarify the believer's relationship with, and responsibilities to, the God of the Universe. Every serious Christian musician will understand and appreciate this book as a valuable resource for maturing the believer and sharing the Gospel."
—**Randall W. Haynes,** Executive Director
Csehy Summer School of Music

"Mark Paulson gives us deep insights to biblical truths. He compares musical concepts with our spiritual life and explains what it means to live under God's authority and be led by the ultimate conductor. This book points out in a beautiful way which position a musician takes in the eternal godly purpose for music. I wish that many readers will be blessed!"
—**Beat Rink,** International Director
CRESCENDO

"A very refreshing view of our relationship with the Creator."
—**Dr. Jim Kraft,** Assistant Chair,
Music Department at Grace College, Director of Orchestra/
Chamber Music Program; Board of directors, Christian
Performing Artists' Fellowship & the MasterWorks Festival

"A wonderful metaphor that should be useful in helping both musicians and composers find God's direction for their lives."
— **Peter Lawrence Alexander**, Author
Writing & Performing Christian Music: God's Plan and Purpose for the Church; How Ravel Orchestrated: Mother Goose Suite

"My cousin Mark Paulson has written this book which presents our Christian life and faith in terms of symbols common to both of us – music and the individuals who produce it. I found it to be most interesting and honoring to our Lord and Savior Jesus Christ, and I recommend it highly."
— **Donald P. Hustad**, Senior Professor
Southern Baptist Theological Seminary, Louisville, KY
Author, *True Worship: Reclaiming the Wonder & Majesty*
Former organist with the Billy Graham Evangelistic Association

"Mark Paulson has emphasized so well in his book *God's Cycle of Music* the importance of giving and dedicating our all in both our spiritual and musical lives. He challenges readers to give their best in their musical endeavors and relationship to Jesus Christ, the Master conductor and composer of our lives."
— **Diane Bish**, "The First Lady of the Organ"
Host, The Joy of Music International Television Series

"Mark Paulson is a sincere follower of Jesus. He, his beautiful wife Sondra, and their wonderful children – Marshall, Elliott and Heidi, are actively engaged in our local church and truly worship as a family. I appreciate the fact that Mark's passion for worship goes beyond his individual role or leadership. He is supportive of anyone who in anyway attempts to see God as the primary audience for their lives. Your life will be impacted by Mark's rich insights on the subject of worship."
— **Terry A. Smith**, Senior Pastor
The Life Christian Church, West Orange, NJ

"To read Mark Paulson's new setting of the age-old story of redemption and salvation is refreshing, reminding us of the simple yet profound mystery of our life in Christ. Set in musical terms, it adds new dimension and expression of the Christian experience for believers and serves as yet another tool for evangelism."
— **Paul Satre,** DMA, Professor of Music
Trinity College, Deerfield, IL
Organist, The Moody Church, Chicago

"Mark Paulson's love for the Lord and his heart for music and musicians truly shine forth in this approachable work. It is his prayer and mine that it will be helpful in encouraging musicians everywhere to deepen their relationship with God through their art and profession."
— **Christopher Harding,** Piano Faculty,
University of Michigan School of Music, Theatre and Dance

"Mr. Paulson has very successfully used his thorough knowledge of both music and spiritual matters to help the rest of us understand how to find our purpose in life. I would recommend this book to anyone searching for a clear and simple explanation of how to do this."
— **Xavier Davis,** jazz pianist, composer and arranger
Member of the Juilliard Jazz faculty

"Mark Paulson uses musical metaphor, Scripture, life illustrations, and music history to explain Biblical truth. His simple presentation will serve as a map for those still seeking, as well as assurance for those 'once lost, but now found.'"
— **Jeremy Kolwinska,** DMA, Chair,
Department of Music, Northwestern College, St. Paul, MN

"What a beautiful metaphor, a rich story of how life must be. Bringing different types of performance to our understanding, Mark Paulson has not only created a masterpiece that continually points to our Maker, but also delivers his writing with the true sensitivity of an artist. By praying constantly throughout this book for each of us to join in *God's Cycle of Music*, Mark has shown us the meaning and purpose for life. 'Sold!'
 —**Dr. Glen Olsen**, Conductor, Composer and Worship Artist
  Associate Faculty, University of Phoenix, Jersey City Center
 Adjunct Faculty, Caspersen School of Graduate Studies, Drew Univ.

Mark Paulson is on to something special. He has given a wonderful gift to all creative types that help us see our spiritual lives as an opus of great sensitivity and power. By setting our walk with God to a beautiful and lyrical analogy, he challenges us to reach a deeper faith and trust in our 'Composer'. I was hooked from Bar #1."
 —**Gary Mauer**, Star of Andrew Lloyd Webber's
 record-breaking Broadway musical, *The Phantom of the Opera*

"In his book *God's Cycle of Music*, Mark Paulson has put into words the intrinsic role of the Spirit of God in the life of every musician whose very life, breath, talent and inspiration is God's Gift! From the depth, yet simplicity of his own experience and trust, Mark reminds us that the key to a meaningful life, career and success is our implicit faith and trust in God's limitless resources."
 —**Nancee Olsen,** MM
 Westminster Choir College; CCM Presbyterian Assoc. of Musicians;
 First prize, Harp, Conservatory of Music/Dramatic Art, Nice, France

"This new resource is a true ministry of encouragement to the reader. The thoughtful insights of Mark's writing have the potential to nurture the life-song in us all."
 —**Joseph Martin**, Director
 Sacred Publications, Shawnee Press

God's Cycle of Music

God's Cycle of Music

A Musician's Explanation of God's Purpose and Meaning for Our Lives

by

Mark Paulson

Hope Publishing House
Pasadena, California

Copyright © 2009 Mark Paulson

All rights reserved.

For information address:

Hope Publishing House
P.O. Box 60008
Pasadena, CA 91116 - U.S.A.
Tel: (626) 792-6123 / Fax: (626) 792-2121
E-mail: hopepub@sbcglobal.net
Web site: http://www.hope-pub.com

Printed on acid-free paper
Cover design – Scott Myles

Library of Congress Cataloging-in-Publication Data

Paulson, Mark, 1958-
 God's cycle of music : a musician's explanation of God's purpose and meaning for out lives / by Mark Paulson.
   p. cm.
 Includes bibliographical references
 ISBN 978-1-932717-18-1 (pbk. : alk. paper)
 1. Christian life. 2. Musicians – Religious life. 3. Music – Religious aspects – Christianity. I. Title
 BV4596.M87P38 2009
 246'.75 – dc22
                                    2009001018

Contents

Acknowledgements 11

1. Prelude 19
2. Explaining God's Cycle of Music 23
3. Identifying the Ultimate Purpose and Meaning for Our Lives: To Know and to Serve the Composer, and to Share in His Honor and Glory Forever in Heaven 35
4. Acquiring a Personal Relationship with the Composer: The Work of Our Agent; Christ Jesus 39
5. Where, When, and How to Participate in God's Cycle of music: The Work of Our Conductor, the Holy Spirit . 45
6. Understanding the Necessary Costs and Requirements in Order For Us to Be Able to Participate in God's Cycle of Music 51
7. Études: Essential Spiritual Disciplines 59
8. Analyzing the Musical Score 75
9. Live to Serve the Composer: Participate in God's Cycle of Music 79

Postlude 85
Bibliography 89
Biblical References 91
Additional Verses for Further Study 93
The Author 95

Acknowledgements

For nearly 50 years, hundreds of people have been influencing my life, helping me to understand the purpose and the meaning for why we are all alive today. The Bible has also been instrumental in revealing to me what it's all about. Through all of this I have come to realize that as a musician, I am a participant in "God's Cycle of Music," so here I would like to use my knowledge of music and the Bible to present my conclusions regarding God's purpose and meaning for our lives here on Earth.

Although written primarily for other musicians, most of the ideas in this book are relevant to everyone. It has only taken two years to write this book, but it has taken an entire lifetime of experiences for me to grasp the concepts that will be presented.

It would be impossible for me to mention everyone who has helped to develop and share these conclusions; however, I would like to express my utmost appreciation to some of them.

My mother, Alice Paulson, taught me that honoring God is the most important thing that I can ever do in my life. She sat with me each and every day while I practiced the piano. Aside from spending an entire lifetime helping others, she taught me that I also need to honor God and offer love and compassion to others by participating in God's Cycle of Music.

My father, Arnold Paulson, taught me to care for everyone, no matter who they were. My dad traveled around the United States and also presided over many different organizations in his local community so he could help others in myriad ways. In 1952 he was named Minnesota's Outstanding Young Man for all of his unselfish accomplishments that made life better for people that he didn't even know.

My lifelong friend, Rev. John Bjorge, taught me that we can share the love of Jesus with people wherever we may be and he showed me how I can include the Composer in any of my daily activities. John also taught me to be humble and to live my life for the Lord. When I was growing up, I was always impressed with the thought: *"What a great God Pastor John has!"* and I will always be grateful for the hundreds of hours he spent with me when I was younger.

Mrs. Rhoda Nelson showed me how I could become a participant in God's Cycle of Music. It was under her tutelage that I was able to learn about the Composer so I could become a child of God. I have had many wonderful piano teachers in my life, but Mrs. Nelson was the one who told me that I needed Jesus Christ to become my Agent and that I needed to follow the guidance from the Conductor, who is the Holy Spirit. Through her influence and instruction, I became a student, learning how to serve the Composer for his honor and glory.

One of my dearest friends was Mrs. Olga Bockes who passed away without ever having a desire to participate in God's Cycle of Music. My countless number of discussions with her helped me to understand why some folk may not be willing to accept the material found in this book. I appreciate all of her contrasting opinions and I miss her very much.

I am also grateful to all of the members of my family, my friends and my relatives who have given me support and theological debates over the years so that I could become more prepared to participate in God's Cycle of Music. Over the years I have been influenced by people at various churches and colleges who have all helped me mature as a Christian. I thank them for their wisdom and their spiritual nurturing.

My wife Sondra and my three children – Marshall, Elliott and Heidi – give me an additional purpose for living every day.

Dr. Neil Gunn-Russell has been a special friend to me and a vital source of spiritual wisdom whenever I have needed his counsel. Rev. Ron Rombough, a wonderful teacher in God's Cycle of Music, has provided me biblical advice for the past 27 years. I also appreciate the suggestions he made to keep this book true and accurate according to the teachings found in the Bible.

I want to thank Dr. Patrick Kavanaugh and the Christian Performing Artists' Fellowship. The Master Works Festival in Winona Lake, Indiana, brings teachers, students, members of the orchestra and the audience in God's Cycle of Music together annually. Each summer the Conductor reveals the Agent to thousands of individuals at the festival so they can come to know and love the Composer. The Conductor also works in the lives of various people who attend the festival so they are able to commit their lives and their talents unto the Composer for his honor and glory. The organizational structure and the intended purposes of this festival were important influences on me when I attempted to gather my thoughts regarding the metaphor of God's Cycle of Music.

Mrs. May Eng taught me that I needed to use every opportunity in my life to serve the Composer for his honor and glory and she made me more aware of the fact that my time here on Earth will soon be over but I still have an amazing future ahead of me because I will be able to live with the Composer forever in heaven.

Mr. Pete Caputo, a great friend and an author, gave me the idea to start writing down my thoughts on God's Cycle of Music. Pete also helps me grow closer to the Composer when I practice the spiritual discipline of fellowship with him.

I want to thank Mrs. Afton Rorvik for reading and editing this book. Her professional advice allowed me to organize and express myself, enabling this book to be more helpful and enjoyable to my readers. I am very grateful to Afton for being willing to share some of her scholarly wisdom with me.

I am especially grateful to Mrs. Julia Craig for doing such an amazing job of assisting me with this work. It would be impossible to express in words my complete appreciation for her encouragement and helpful suggestions regarding this project. If this book has an impact on the lives of anyone, it will be due to the assistance that Julia offered me in expressing these thoughts.

Faith Annette Sand and the Hope Publishing House were willing to accept my book and put it into print. I can not begin to thank them enough for everything that they have done in order to make this book possible.

It is important for me to acknowledge my gratitude for the trials that I have had to face at various times throughout my life. These trials tested my faith so that I could understand my purpose and my meaning for being alive.

I am also very thankful to God for the Bible. It says in *James 1:2-4:* *"Consider it pure joy, my brothers, whenever you face trials of many kinds, because you know that the testing of your faith develops perseverance. Perseverance must finish its work so that you may be mature and complete, not lacking anything."*

My greatest appreciation is to God – the Composer, the Agent and the Conductor in God's Cycle of Music. I am so grateful to the Composer for making it possible for me to be alive. He also continues to watch over me so that I can fulfill my purpose and my meaning for being in this world. I want to give thanks to the Agent for dying on the cross for me so that the penalty for my sins could be paid in full and for negotiating my contract with the Composer so that I could actually have a personal relationship with him. I want to thank the Conductor for introducing me to the Agent. I am grateful to him for his spiritual wisdom and for the guidance he constantly gives me each and every day of my life as I continue to participate in God's Cycle of Music.

We are not able to understand the purpose and the meaning for our lives on our own. God works in us and he also uses many individuals so that we can eventually comprehend the plan he has intended for our lives. I will always be grateful to everyone who has helped me to understand God's specific plan for my life. Now I pray that this book will help you to know God's specific plan for your life as well.

1

Prelude

Psalm 8:3-6: When I consider your heavens, the work of your fingers, the moon and the stars, which you have set in place, what is man that you are mindful of him, the son of man that you care for him? You made him a little lower than the heavenly beings and crowned him with glory and honor. You made him ruler over the works of your hands; you put everything under his feet.

I believe most of us want to find a purpose and a meaning for our lives. Many musicians dedicate their entire lives to music in order to perfect their talents and achieve the personal goals they intend to accomplish. Becoming a professional musician requires this kind of commitment, but I believe there is even a greater commitment that every individual needs to make while living here on this planet. This commitment is to God. God has a specific plan for each and every one of us.

In offering my explanation of God's plan for our lives, I intend to use the metaphor which I have referred to – God's Cycle of Music. If we are willing to make this commitment to God, we will be able to know and experience God's ultimate purpose and meaning for our lives.

When I was four years old, I asked my mother for piano lessons. Now, for nearly 45 years, I have been playing or teaching people how to play the piano. I have spent my entire life developing skills that allow me to be a professional musician. Even though I make my living as a piano teacher and as a performer, I have come to realize that teaching and playing the piano is not my most important purpose nor the meaning for being in this world. However, my experiences in music have helped me to understand how I can fulfill God's intended purpose and meaning for my life.

There were several times during my pilgrimage when I believed playing and teaching music was my only purpose for being alive. I would ask myself, "What would happen if I could not use my skills in music to accomplish my own personal goals? Would my life have any value at all if I were not a musician?"

Perhaps you have had similar thoughts regarding your own unique talents and abilities. Fortunately I have come to realize that my ultimate purpose in life is simply to know God and to serve him in everything that I do and say. Now music is primarily important in my life because it allows me to serve God in a way that I believe brings honor and glory to him.

If anyone attempts to find the purpose and the meaning for their life, they will continue to search for answers until they realize that they exist primarily to love and to serve the One who has created them. The Composer has made us. We are his Music. When we understand and accept this, we will know the purpose and the meaning for our lives and what we should be doing with the talents that we are capable of offering unto him.

Writing this book is just one of the ways in which I have been able to participate in God's Cycle of Music. This project was undertaken so that you can know God's divine purpose and meaning for your life. This purpose is the reason why we are all alive. He has revealed this purpose and this meaning to me and now I pray that he will reveal it to you. Are you interested in knowing God's purpose and meaning for your life today?

2

Explaining God's Cycle of Music

Romans 8:28: And we know that in all things God works for the good of those who love him, who have been called according to his purpose.

God's Cycle of Music is a metaphor intended to explain God's purpose and meaning for our lives. There are several different parts to God's Cycle of Music but they all work together to show how God, the Composer, uses the people that he has created in order to receive honor and glory for himself.

The divisions in the Cycle are: the Composer, the Teacher, the Student, the Members of the Orchestra and the Audience. There are also five other components that are essential in the explanation of God's purpose and meaning for our lives: the Music, the Agent, the Conductor, the Critic's Review and the Rewards in Heaven.

The Cycle has continued to spin around and around ever since God created the world. All of us can know our intended purpose and meaning for our lives if we are willing to commit our lives unto the Composer and if we are willing to participate in God's Cycle of Music.

The Composer and His Music

God's Cycle of Music begins with the Composer – the Creator of everything. His Music is everything he ever made. God's motive for creating the world was based on his desire to receive honor and glory and to share this honor and glory in heaven with every individual he created who would be willing to commit their life unto him.

There is only one Composer in God's Cycle of Music. The Composer receives all the honor and the glory. God is the only one worthy to receive this praise. One of the greatest writers of music in the 20th Century completely understood his position in God's Cycle of Music. Igor Stravinsky dedicated his Symphony of Psalms, "to the glory of God." When someone once asked him where his inspiration came from, he said, "Only God can create. I make music from music" (Kavanaugh 2000).

Everything we do must always be done exclusively for the glory and the honor of the Composer; no matter who we are or how famous we may be.

The Agent

The Composer has created each and every one of us, but our sins prevent us from experiencing a personal relationship with him. God could not have a relationship with us until the penalty for our sins had been completely paid. God sent his one and only Son, Jesus Christ, to make this payment for our sins.

Jesus Christ is our Agent. His sacrifice on the cross allowed him to be able to go before the Composer and tell him that the penalty for our sins has been paid in full. Jesus died on the cross for us so that we could have a personal relationship with God. He is the only one who can ever go before the Composer and represent us. Without Jesus, we would never be able to have a personal relationship with the Composer or be able to experience the ultimate purpose and meaning for our lives.

The Conductor

The Holy Spirit is the Conductor in God's Cycle of Music. The Holy Spirit is the one who leads us to the Agent, Christ Jesus, so that we can have a personal relationship with the Composer. The Conductor also directs the participants in God's Cycle of Music so that they can know where, when and how to serve the Composer.

The Teacher

Anyone who is willing to commit their life unto the Composer, through the guidance of the Conductor and the representation of the Agent, is given the opportunity to participate in God's Cycle of Music.

One of the ways in which we can participate in God's Cycle of Music is by becoming a Teacher. Teachers are given the responsibility of educating new believers about the Composer or of helping more mature Christians establish a deeper relationship with him so they can be more prepared to fulfill the assignments that they will receive from the Conductor.

The Student

New believers are called Students in God's Cycle of Music. Students have been given spiritual guidance from the Conductor so they can comprehend and accept God's special plan for their lives. Students are taught by Teachers so they can eventually serve the Composer by becoming Teachers or Members of the Orchestra.

The Members of the Orchestra

Members of the Orchestra perform for the Audience. They do this by caring for the various needs of the Audience and by telling them about the Composer and his intended plan for their lives. The Members of the Orchestra also encourage individuals from the Audience to respond to the guidance and the direction from the Conductor so that they can come to know and commit their lives unto the Composer.

The Members of the Orchestra must always be led by the Conductor in order to be effective servants for the Composer. They must also rely on the Word of God so that they can learn how to serve him better.

The Audience and Our Purpose and Meaning in Life

Every individual that the Composer created is part of the Audience. The Audience has been created so they can offer praise and adoration unto the Composer. However, if people do not know the Composer, they are unable to accomplish this purpose and this meaning for their lives. In order for them to be able to comprehend and establish a personal relationship with the Composer, the Conductor must guide them to the Agent so that the Agent can make this relationship possible and they can put their faith in him.

After people in the Audience ask the Agent to negotiate a deal with the Composer on their behalf – so they can have a personal relationship with him – the Composer wants them to participate in God's Cycle of Music.

Everyone who commits their life unto the Composer will continue to remain as part of the Audience; however, this commitment will in the end allow them to be able to understand God's intended purpose and meaning for their lives. They will also be able to offer their praise and adoration unto the Composer for everything that he has done.

The Critic's Review and the Rewards in Heaven

At the end of the final performance on Earth, the Agent will come to take all of the participants in God's Cycle of Music to heaven. This is where they will live forever with him.

When a performance is over, a review is usually presented. The Composer will be giving his own review at the end of the world. The Composer's review is the most important review we will ever receive. We must be given a favorable review in order to be allowed to live in heaven forever. If our names are written in the Composer's review, we will receive a "crown of righteousness."

This reward is only possible if the Conductor guides us to the Agent so that we can have a personal relationship with the Composer. The ultimate purpose and meaning for our lives will come to pass if we are allowed to live and reign in heaven with the Conductor, the Agent and the Composer forever and ever – sharing in their glory for everything that has been done.

This chapter was written in order to present God's Cycle of Music. The metaphor provides a brief explanation of God's purpose and meaning for our lives from the perspective of a musician. However, a complete explanation of the purpose and the meaning for our lives is found in the Bible. I pray that this metaphor will inspire you to study the Bible and give you a greater desire to know the Composer better. I also pray that the following chapters will motivate all of us to serve the Composer in various ways, through our participation in God's Cycle of Music, for his honor and glory.

3

Identifying the Ultimate Purpose and Meaning for Our Lives: To Know and Serve the Composer and Share in His Honor and Glory Forever in Heaven

Revelation 4:11: You are worthy, our Lord and God, to receive glory and honor and power, for you created all things, and by your will they were created and have their being.

Why do people search to find a purpose and a meaning for their lives? I believe there is emptiness in our lives that can only be filled when we come to know our Maker. We were all created in the image of God but sin separates us from him. So how can we possibly have a relationship with God if there is sin in our lives?

God sent his one and only son, Jesus Christ, to die on a cross to pay the penalty for our sins. Only Jesus' payment on the cross can make it possible for us to know the Composer. God has provided a way for us to have a personal relationship with him but many are reluctant to accept his offer. We all look for other purposes and meanings for being alive but, unless we have a desire to know the Composer and to serve him, we will never be able to experience our ultimate purpose and meaning for our lives in this world or the world to come.

How can we find our purpose and our meaning in life? We can only find these answers when the Holy Spirit convicts our hearts and we accept the payment that Jesus Christ paid for us on the cross. We need the Conductor to lead us to our Agent. Once we put our faith in Christ Jesus, the Composer wants us to serve him for his honor and glory instead of living our lives to satisfy our own personal desires.

We also need to tell other individuals about Jesus and what he did for them on the cross. This is one of the primary reasons why we have been created. However, this is also one of the primary reasons why so many of us will conclude that the purpose and the meaning for our lives are impossible to grasp. We are unwilling to give up the desires that we have for our own lives in exchange for the intended purposes that God established for us when he created the world.

Being successful and achieving our own personal accomplishments can be exciting and enjoyable, but this is not God's primary purpose and meaning for giving us life. We will not find the ultimate purpose for our lives by accomplishing great things for our own honor and glory. God has given us talents so we can use them for him. However, before we are able to use our talents for God's honor and glory, we must have a personal relationship with the Composer.

The Composer has an intended purpose for your life. Today you may not feel important at all or you might believe you are the most important person in the world. However, the only thing that really matters is what the Composer thinks about you.

It is impossible to put into words exactly what the Composer truly thinks about any of us but, through spiritual understanding that comes from the guidance of the Conductor and through the shed blood that Jesus Christ paid for us on the cross, we can experience a personal relationship with the Composer and understand his divine purpose and meaning for our lives. Once we commit our lives unto him, the Composer wants us to use our talents and our lives for his honor and glory.

There are many ways in which we can serve God. We can write a symphony for his honor or perform a wonderful piece of music for his glory. We can become a Teacher so that our Students can learn how to use their talents. We can tell the Audience about the Composer. We can worship the Composer and give him praise for everything that he has done. It is possible to serve God in many different ways but we must always be led by the Conductor so that we can know exactly what the Composer wants for us to do.

Do you have a personal relationship with the Composer? This is the first thing that must occur in order for you to know the purpose and the meaning for your life. Do you believe that the Composer has a specific plan for your life? If he does have a specific plan for your life, would you be willing to sacrifice your own personal desires so that he could receive the honor and the glory from the talents that you are able to offer unto him? Are you willing to accept the payment that Jesus paid for you on the cross?

Jesus wants to become your Agent. If Jesus is not your Agent, I pray that the Conductor will lead you to him today. Are you willing to commit your life unto him so that you can experience God's ultimate purpose and meaning for your life? Will you receive a favorable review from him so that you can live in heaven with the Composer, the Agent, and the Conductor forever?

Take time to honestly answer these questions. You must be able to answer these questions in ways that are acceptable to God if you want to know and experience his purpose and meaning for your life.

4

Acquiring a Personal Relationship with the Composer – The Work of Our Agent: Christ Jesus

Romans 5:1-2: Therefore, since we have been justified through faith, we have peace with God through our Lord Jesus Christ, through whom we have gained access by faith into this grace in which we now stand. And we rejoice in the hope of the glory of God.

A couple of years ago, I asked one of my piano students to sing one of the phrases in her music. When she sang for me, I discovered that she had a beautiful singing voice. I am not a vocal instructor so I encouraged my student and her mother to look for someone who was qualified to help her develop this talent.

The following week I was delighted to find out that my piano student was starting to take voice lessons from a highly trained vocal teacher who also acknowledged that my piano student was a gifted singer. After a few months of lessons, this student wanted to audition for one of the leading roles in *The Lion King* on Broadway.

She had everything that was necessary in order for her to get the part – except that she did not have an agent. Her voice was absolutely perfect for the role, but she was not offered the job because she needed someone to represent her. However, a few weeks later, my piano student had one of the leading roles in *The Lion King* because she was being represented by one of the finest talent agents in New York City.

Before we can ever participate in God's Cycle of Music, it is essential for Jesus Christ to become our Agent. Sin prevents us from having a personal relationship with the Composer. We could never obtain a personal relationship with the Composer on our own. Only our Agent could pay the penalty for our sins so that we could experience a relationship with the Composer.

This is what our Agent did for us when he died on the cross. Everyone must be represented by Jesus if they want to participate in God's Cycle of Music. This is also essential if we want to spend eternity in heaven with the Composer.

Some people believe that everyone goes to heaven when they die. This is simply not true. God will not allow anyone into heaven if the penalty for their sins has not been paid in full. Jesus had to die on the cross because God can not tolerate sin. He could not even have a relationship with Jesus while he was hanging on the cross. It says in Matthew 27:46, *"About the ninth hour Jesus cried out in a loud voice, 'Eloi, Eloi, lama sabachthani?'— which means, "My God, my God, why have you forsaken me?"*

We can not enter into heaven if our sins have not been forgiven. If Jesus is not our Agent, we will not be allowed to live forever with the Composer.

Other people believe that they have never done anything that could possibly be offensive to God. The Bible clearly states that everyone has sinned and has fallen short of God's expectations. It says in Romans 3:23, *"For all have sinned and fall short of the glory of God."*

Some people believe that they have committed sins that can never be forgiven. Their entire lives have been filled with pain and suffering because they are convinced that God could never forgive them for the acts they have committed.

The entire Bible is a book of love and forgiveness. The Bible says in Isaiah 1:18, *"'Come now, let us reason together,' says the Lord. 'Though your sins are like scarlet, they shall be as white as snow; though they are red as crimson, they shall be like wool.'"*

None of us will ever be able to understand why God loves and forgives us. However, God is willing to love and forgive anyone if they will come unto him. This is why all of us need Jesus. Jesus is our Agent. He makes it possible for us to have a relationship with the Composer.

We all know that an agent is someone who represents an individual so that certain agreements can be made between all of the negotiating parties. The agent negotiates the terms of the agreements in the best interest of the person whom they are representing. It is usually impossible for an individual to reach a satisfactory settlement with the other parties that are involved in these kinds of situations without the representation that an agent can provide.

Jesus is the only agent qualified to represent us before the Composer because he is the only one who can stand sinless in front of him. Jesus is also worthy to represent us because he has paid the penalty for our sins. Above everything else, Jesus is God.

God could not tolerate sin so he personally had to die on the cross for us. We could not possibly make this payment on our own. We may be very talented and willing to serve the Composer but we will never be worthy enough to stand before him and negotiate our own eternal destiny.

Jesus must become our Agent if we want to have a personal relationship with the Composer and if we want to be qualified to participate in God's Cycle of Music.

Jesus will stand before the Composer on our behalf and tell him that we have met all of the requirements that are necessary in order for him to be able to use us.

If you still have not offered your life unto God, I pray that the Holy Spirit will convict your heart so that Jesus can become your Agent today.

John 14:6 tells us: *"Jesus answered, 'I am the way and the truth and the life. No one comes to the Father except through me.'"*

5

Where, When and How to Participate in God's Cycle of Music: The Work of Our Conductor, the Holy Spirit

Romans 8:12-17: Therefore, brothers, we have an obligation—but it is not to the sinful nature, to live according to it. For if you live according to the sinful nature, you will die; but if by the Spirit you put to death the misdeeds of the body, you will live, because those who are led by the Spirit of God are sons of God. For you did not receive a spirit that makes you a slave again to fear, but you received the Spirit of sonship. And by him we cry, 'Abba, Father.' The Spirit himself testifies with our spirit that we are God's children. Now if we are children, then we are heirs—heirs of God and co-heirs with Christ, if indeed we share in his sufferings in order that we may also share in his glory.

My wife and I recently went to Tanglewood in Massachusetts to hear a concert. An orchestra performed three pieces under the direction of three different conductors. The first two conductors received a nice but a short round of applause for their direction and their leadership. The final conductor moved his baton in a way that caused the musicians to sound like one of the finest orchestras in the world. It was amazing to witness the transformation that took place among these musicians through the guidance of this one special conductor.

The Conductor can make all of the difference in your life as well. He can lead you to the Agent so that you can have a personal relationship with the Composer. His guidance can cause you to become a "spiritual virtuoso" and your life can be transformed into something that is far greater than you could ever imagine. The Conductor also guides and directs everything that the Composer has created so that the Composer can receive honor and glory for the things that he has made.

The Composer has a specific purpose for our lives so he needed to provide a way for us to find it. That is why we need to be guided by the Conductor. The Conductor reveals the Composer's specific purpose for our lives to us. Without the Holy Spirit, God's purpose and meaning for our lives would continue to remain a mystery. Without the Holy Spirit, it would be impossible for any of us to ever understand how we could experience a personal relationship with God or be able to know where, when and how to serve him. However, through the spiritual direction that comes from the Conductor, we can know exactly what the Composer wants for us to do with our lives.

It is very important to notice that the words Jesus spoke to those whom he was with could not be completely understood until the time when the Composer chose to reveal this message to them. For example, Jesus told his disciples that he was going to die and rise again from the tomb after just three days. The Bible says in Matthew 20:17-19, *"Now as Jesus was going up to Jerusalem, he took the twelve disciples aside and said to them, 'We are going up to Jerusalem, and the Son of Man will be betrayed to the chief priests and the teachers of the law. They will condemn him to death and will turn him over to the Gentiles to be mocked and flogged and crucified. On the third day he will be raised to life!'"*

However, even after witnessing myriad miracles and being able to be in the presence of Jesus every day, none of his disciples sat at his grave with any hope at all of observing his resurrection. Where were the 5,000 folk who were fed with just a few fish and some bread? Where were the individuals whom Jesus raised from the dead? Why weren't they waiting at the tomb to see if Jesus could raise himself? Where were the people who worshiped him on Palm Sunday? Was all hope lost at the cross?

Even Mary, who was one of his closest friends, did not recognize him at his tomb. Two men did not know who he was while they walked with Jesus on the road to Emmaus. These men told Jesus that their Messiah was dead; even after they had been informed that the body of Jesus was missing from the tomb. Why couldn't they recognize Jesus? Why couldn't anyone believe that Jesus would return from the grave?

We can only know the Composer and have a personal relationship with him after the Conductor opens our hearts and our minds so that the message of the Agent can be revealed to us.

If you want to know the purpose and the meaning for your life, the Conductor must reveal it to you by introducing you to the Agent. The Agent will meet with the Composer on your behalf so that you can become eligible to serve him. In order to serve the Composer, we must receive the power that can only come from the Conductor. That is why it says in Acts 1:8, *"But you will receive power when the Holy Spirit comes on you; and you will be my witnesses in Jerusalem, and in all Judea and Samaria, and to the ends of the earth."*

In Acts chapter two, the Holy Spirit came to live and reign in the physical bodies of the new believers. Immediately these individuals were able to know God and serve him in ways that were never possible before.

Once we have a personal relationship with the Composer, the Conductor wants to direct our lives and guide us in everything that we do and say when we participate in God's Cycle of Music. However, it is important to understand that the Holy Spirit will not usually reveal to us the Composer's entire purpose and plans for our lives all at once. The Conductor normally will only reveal to us small portions of his plan at a time. This is done so that we will remain dependent on the guidance from the Conductor in everything that we do and say when we serve the Composer.

I encourage every participant in God's Cycle of Music to ask the Conductor for an opportunity to be of service to the Composer right now. We must also be aware that God will probably give us assignments that we would never request on our own. However, we need to be willing to serve the Composer whenever we are being directed by the Conductor.

Occasionally we will wonder if a particular assignment has come to us from God. One of the lessons that I teach my piano students is that there is a significant difference between "hearing and listening." I believe that we all hear many things every day but it takes much more concentration and effort to be able to listen. Many of us will believe that we hear assignments from God but we will only be able to determine if they are "divine assignments" and be able to know if they are from the Holy Spirit when we make the extra effort to listen closely to him.

In order to listen to the Holy Spirit, we will need to quiet our hearts so that we can know his voice. The

Conductor provides spiritual discernment so that we can determine if the Composer is speaking to us. It says in 1 Corinthians 14:33, *"For God is not a God of disorder but of peace."* If we are confused about certain things in our lives, we must study the scriptures and ask God for his peace. If we do not have peace in our hearts, we should assume that it is probably not from the Composer.

I can not begin to express in words how important the Conductor's guidance is in order for us to determine where, when and how to serve the Composer. When I listen to the Conductor and seek his direction, he gives me the right words to say to people. My heart is also convicted by the Conductor whenever I do things that are unpleasing to the Composer. He helps me to understand the Bible and he makes me aware of God's love. The Conductor guides me in every aspect of my life whenever I am willing to follow his directions. I can not be an effective participant in God's Cycle of Music without the guidance from the Holy Spirit.

If anyone wants to find the purpose and the meaning for their life, they must be willing to allow the Conductor to be their guide. It is my prayer that the Holy Spirit is, or that he will become, the guide of your life today.

6

Understanding the Necessary Costs and Requirements in Order for Us to Be Able to Participate in God's Cycle of Music

Matthew 16:24-27: Then Jesus said to his disciples, "If anyone would come after me, he must deny himself and take up his cross and follow me. For whoever wants to save his life will lose it, but whoever loses his life for me will find it. What good will it be for a man if he gains the whole world, yet forfeits his soul? Or what can a man give in exchange for his soul? For the Son of Man is going to come in his Father's glory with his angels, and then he will reward each person according to what he has done."

When I was seven years old, I went to an auction in my home town. I had my entire life savings of fifty cents safely tucked in my front pocket. Every time the auctioneer held up an item, I shouted out, "fifty cents." Everyone laughed as each item quickly received a higher bid. Finally, just before the auction was about to end, the auctioneer held up a baseball glove. I shouted out, "fifty cents." The auctioneer immediately looked at me and said, "Sold." Everyone cheered and congratulated me as I jumped for joy around the room with my new baseball glove.

What does it cost to be able to participate in God's Cycle of Music? In order to be able to participate in the Cycle, we need to have a personal relationship with the Composer. It is only possible to have a personal relationship with the Composer through faith in Christ Jesus and by God's grace.

It says in Romans 3:22-24, *"This righteousness from God comes through faith in Jesus Christ to all who believe. There is no difference, for all have sinned and fall short of the glory of God, and are justified freely by his grace through the redemption that came by Christ Jesus."* It also says in Ephesians 2:8-9, *"For it is by grace you have been saved, through faith—and this not from yourselves, it is the gift of God—not by works, so that no one can boast."*

A personal relationship with God is a free gift that we could never afford. The Composer knows that we only have fifty cents in our "spiritual pockets," but he wants to have a relationship with us if we will simply put our faith in Jesus and accept his gift of grace. If we will do this, he will look at what we have to offer, meet with our Agent, and immediately say to us, "Sold."

There are many costs involved in having a personal relationship with the Composer and being able to participate in God's Cycle of Music. The most expensive cost occurred long before we were even born. The Bible says that in order for God to have a relationship with sinners, which refers to every human being that has ever lived on the face of the earth, he had to offer his one and only Son to die on the cross. John 3:16 says, *"For God so loved the world that he gave his one and only Son, that whoever believes in him shall not perish but have eternal life."* It also says in Romans 5:8, *"But God demonstrates his own love for us in this: While we were still sinners, Christ died for us."* Jesus sacrificed his very own life for you and for me.

Once we begin to have a personal relationship with the Composer, we are expected to dedicate our own lives unto him for his honor and glory. This dedication implies that we are willing to participate in God's Cycle of Music in a way that is pleasing to him.

If we want to participate in God's Cycle of Music, we must be willing to accept the following costs: submit to the guidance from the Conductor in order to know where, when and how to serve the Composer; have purity in our actions and in our thoughts; have compassion for the needs of others; study the Bible; observe spiritual disciplines; and have a sincere desire to live our lives primarily for the Lord.

Serving the Composer could cost us everything that we will ever acquire in this world. Are you willing to accept these costs so that you can know God's purpose and meaning for your life? I can assure you that if you will offer your life unto the Composer, you will be happier than that little boy who jumped around the room with his new baseball glove after he heard the auctioneer say to him, "Sold."

Fritz Kreisler was one of the greatest violinists who have ever played the instrument. He was also a famous composer who lived from 1875-1962. At the end of one of his concerts, a woman came up to him and said, "Sir, I'd give my life to play like that." Fritz Kreisler responded by saying, "Madam, I did" (Delker 2006). Mr. Kreisler knew he had to devote his entire life to the violin in order to accomplish the things that he wanted to achieve.

Johann Sebastian Bach (1685-1750) was a person who spent his entire life composing music so that God could receive honor and glory. *Soli Deo Gloria,* "to the only God be glory," was Bach's motto throughout his entire lifetime. For this reason he wrote all of his compositions on staff paper that contained the watermark *Jesu, juva!* "Jesus, help!" When he completed his compositions, he would sign his works, S.D.G. *Soli Deo Gloriato* "To the only God be glory" (Farstad 1996).

Today, if we want to hear all of Bach's music that has been preserved, we will need to listen to 155 CDs (Brilliant Classics 2006). We must also consider the possibility that Bach probably wrote much more music that has been lost over the years. Bach worked endlessly throughout his entire lifetime in order to write music so that God could receive honor and glory for the work that he was able to offer unto him.

Johann Sebastian Bach and Fritz Kreisler both understood the sacrifices that they needed to make in order for each of them to accomplish their goals. Their dedication is almost too intense for me to comprehend. However, God expects this kind of commitment from everyone who intends to serve him. Johann Sebastian Bach and Fritz Kreisler were willing to sacrifice everything that they had in life in order to accomplish their goals. Are we willing to dedicate our own lives unto the Composer for his honor and glory? Johann Sebastian Bach committed his entire life for the purpose of *Soli Deo Gloria.*

I have committed my own life for the purpose of *Soli Deo Gloria* as well so that God can receive honor and glory for everything that I am able to offer unto him. This book has been dedicated unto him so that he can use it for his own purposes. I have committed my family and my finances unto the Lord. Everything that I do today and in the future needs to be done exclusively for God's honor and glory. I understand that this requires a complete sacrifice of my own life unto him. There is nothing that I can withhold.

Jesus died on the cross for me because I am a sinner. He paid the penalty for my sins because he loved me. The Conductor made me aware of the Composer's free gift of grace and how I could have a relationship with him. This was the only way in which I could have ever been able to understand the purpose and the meaning for my life. Today I am completely dependent on the Holy Spirit for his guidance, in order to keep my commitment unto the Composer, because this would be impossible for me to sustain without him.

Jesus left his throne in heaven to die on the cross because he loved me. He would have made that sacrifice if I was the only person to ever live here on Earth. However, every believer can rejoice in the fact that Jesus has also made that payment for them as well. If Jesus was willing to do this, I believe that we need to be willing to commit our own lives unto the Composer.

I would like to share a hymn with you that I found in a very old Baptist hymnal. The lyrics for this hymn, written in 1872, must have been written by someone who truly desired to commit their life unto the Composer. Their love for the Composer can be seen in every line that they wrote. They obviously understood their purpose and their meaning for living in this world.

Had I Ten Thousand Thousand Tongues

O Lord, if in the book of life
My worthless name shall stand,
In fairest characters inscribed
By thine unerring hand,
Then I to thee in sweetest strains,
Will grateful anthems raise;
But life's too short, my powers too weak,
To utter half thy praise.
Had I ten thousand thousand tongues,
Not one should silent be;
Had I ten thousand thousand hearts,
I'd give them all to thee.

—Dr. G. M. Garrett (1902:347).

Are you willing to dedicate your life and your talents unto the Composer for his honor and glory? The Bible says that Jesus sacrificed his very own life for us. In Philippians 2:6-8 it says, *"Who, being in very nature God, did not consider equality with God something to be grasped, but made himself nothing, taking the very nature of a servant, being made in human likeness. And being found in appearance as a man, he humbled himself and became obedient to death—even death on a cross!"*

Jesus had to leave his home in heaven and humble himself by coming to Earth, so that he could take the form of a human being. For over thirty years he experienced life in some of the same ways in which we experience life each and every day. He also had to suffer and die on the cross so that the penalty for our sins could be paid in full. This was the "real" cost that was necessary so that, with just fifty cents in our "spiritual pockets," our hope for a relationship with the Composer could be possible, and he could say to us, "Sold."

If Jesus was willing to do this, I pray that you will be willing to offer him anything that you have for his honor and glory.

7

Études:
Essential Spiritual Disciplines

> *1 Peter 1:13: Therefore, prepare your minds for action; be self-controlled; set your hope fully on the grace to be given you when Jesus Christ is revealed.*

Everyone needs to be prepared before they can become effective participants in God's Cycle of Music. Musicians should never give a performance until they are ready to go in front of an audience.

Preparation is even more essential in order to serve the Composer. If we want to be prepared to participate in God's Cycle of Music, we will need to practice the following spiritual disciplines: baptism, Bible study, fellowship, fasting, worship, stewardship, prayer, confession and communion. Every believer must continue to apply these études to their own lives in order to remain strong when they serve the Lord.

If someone attempts to participate in God's Cycle of Music without these spiritual disciplines, they will begin to feel disconnected from God. If they refuse to practice these études, they will eventually stop participating in God's Cycle of Music all together. Every participant in God's Cycle of Music needs to practice the following spiritual disciplines.

Baptism

Romans 6:3-4: Or don't you know that all of us who were baptized into Christ Jesus were baptized into his death? We were therefore buried with him through baptism into death in order that, just as Christ was raised from the dead through the glory of the Father, we too may live a new life.

Baptism is the first spiritual discipline that a person needs to practice after they have committed their life unto the Composer. I believe that it is significant to notice that Jesus was baptized at the beginning of his ministry. Baptism was not necessary for his salvation but he wanted to be baptized before he began his mission.

Baptism is expected from everyone who desires to participate in God's Cycle of Music. It is a public confession that identifies us with the death, the burial, and the resurrection of Jesus Christ. Being baptized is also a public display of our own humility before God and before other individuals.

If you are a participant in God's Cycle of Music and you have not been baptized, I encourage you to fulfill this spiritual discipline immediately. Baptism may be one of your greatest opportunities to proclaim your love for the Composer to others. Every servant of the Composer needs to be baptized if they are living a new life and they desire to be used by him.

Bible Study

Psalm 119:11: I have hidden your word in my heart that I might not sin against you.

If we are going to be prepared to serve the Composer, it is essential for us to study the Bible for it is God's Holy Word. It allows us to learn about him and it shows us how we can participate in God's Cycle of Music. It also teaches us how we need to live our lives so that we can honor him with the things that we do or say.

Every participant in God's Cycle of Music is expected to study the Bible throughout their entire lifetime so that they can remain obedient unto God and develop their relationship with the Composer. It is also very important to memorize God's Word.

Read God's Word every day so that you can grow closer to him and be able to share the Good News with others when you participate in God's Cycle of Music.

Fellowship

Matthew 18:19-20: Again, I tell you that if two of you on earth agree about anything you ask for, it will be done for you by my Father in heaven. For where two or three come together in my name, there am I with them.

One of the most neglected spiritual disciplines in our busy world today is fellowship. We need to pray and study the Bible on a regular basis with other believers. We need to memorize scripture together and share our concerns with one another so that we can face the trials that life will bring. We also need to be accountable to one another so that we will not get involved in various sinful behaviors.

It says in Proverbs 27:17, *"As iron sharpens iron, so one man sharpens another."* Ask the Conductor to lead you to someone today. I encourage you to find at least one other individual whom you can have fellowship with if you do not have anyone at this time.

Fasting

Matthew 17:19-21: Then the disciples came to Jesus in private and asked, "Why couldn't we drive it out?" He replied, "Because you have so little faith. I tell you the truth, if you have faith as small as a mustard seed, you can say to this mountain, 'Move from here to there' and it will move. Nothing will be impossible for you. But this kind does not go out except by prayer and fasting."

Fasting is another important spiritual discipline that draws us closer to God. When people fast, they go for a period of time without food and sometimes even water in order to seek spiritual nourishment from the Composer.

God wants us to take time for prayer and fasting so that we can obtain the spiritual strength that will be necessary in order for us to serve him. Food is important to everyone because it provides nourishment for our bodies. Without food, we would all die. However, we also need to obtain spiritual nourishment that comes from fasting. Every person who commits their life unto God needs to take time to fast as part of their regular spiritual diet so that they can receive this essential nourishment from the Lord. Fasting also reminds us that we need to be completely dependent upon the Composer.

Worship

Psalm 95:6-7: Come, let us bow down in worship, let us kneel before the Lord our Maker; for he is our God and we are the people of his pasture, the flock under his care.

Worship is a very important spiritual discipline. Worship shows reverence, adoration and honor to God. We are also instructed to bow down before him. "But a deeper study of worship shows that it is more a thing of the heart and mind than a physical action or a position. Perhaps we can say that worship means having a bowed-down head and heart as we adore and revere our Maker! It is an attitude of total and unconditional surrender to the One we call our Master, our Lord, and our God. Mere words and actions are not enough" *(Worship God!)*.

Many people will drift away from God and into activities that are evil because they neglect to worship the Composer. Worship makes us stronger so that we can avoid falling into the traps that Satan will put in front of us.

I believe that the primary intention of every worshiper should be to praise God for who he is. Our worship should not be conditional on the blessings that he offers unto us. God loves us and blesses us in many different ways but this is not the primary reason why we should ever worship him. We simply need to humble ourselves and worship God because he is worthy of our praise.

It is also important to continue to worship him when life is difficult. Worship is not conditional on our own individual circumstances. Worship needs to be given unto the Composer simply because he is worthy of anything that we can offer unto him.

Worship is an essential spiritual discipline. Our strength will be renewed when we offer our praise and our adoration unto God. If we want to go out into the world and serve the Lord, it is absolutely necessary for us to offer our worship unto him. We can do this wherever we are—each and every day of our lives. If we will do this, we will become stronger and more prepared to participate in God's Cycle of Music.

Stewardship

2 Corinthians 9:6-8: Remember this: Whoever sows sparingly will also reap sparingly, and whoever sows generously will also reap generously. Each man should give what he has decided in his heart to give, not reluctantly or under compulsion, for God loves a cheerful giver. And God is able to make all grace abound to you, so that in all things at all times, having all that you need, you will abound in every good work.

The Bible has more references about money and what to do with our money than any other topic; including love. Jesus spoke several times about money and how to use it. If we desire to participate in God's Cycle of Music, we will need to understand and practice the spiritual discipline of stewardship.

Stewardship allows us to demonstrate our love to God and our love to our neighbors. It is also a way for us to obey the two most important commandments that were ever written. It says in Mark 12:28-31, *"One of the teachers of the law came and heard them debating. Noticing that Jesus had given them a good answer, he asked him, 'Of all the commandments, which is the most important?' 'The most important one,' answered Jesus, 'is this: "Hear, O Israel, the*

Lord our God, the Lord is one. Love the Lord your God with all your heart and with all your soul and with all your mind and with all your strength." The second is this: "Love your neighbor as yourself." There is no commandment greater than these."

We need to understand that everything that we have is from the Lord. It is from him and for him. God allows us to use the things that he has given to us in order to help others who are in need. If money is more important to us than being faithful servants to the Composer, we will not be able to become effective witnesses for him. We need to be willing to offer any of our possessions unto God so that we can truly know in our own hearts that he is our most valuable treasure.

It is also important to mention that we need to be faithful stewards to the places where we are being spiritually fed. The Bible says in 1 Timothy 5:17-18, *"The elders who direct the affairs of the church well are worthy of double honor, especially those whose work is preaching and teaching. For the Scripture says, 'Do not muzzle the ox while it is treading out the grain,' and 'The worker deserves his wages.'"*

I believe that if we will honor God with the gifts that he has given to us, we will be blessed by him and be more prepared to serve the Composer when we participate in God's Cycle of Music.

Prayer

James 5:16: Therefore confess your sins to each other and pray for each other so that you may be healed. The prayer of a righteous man is powerful and effective.

Prayer is a very important spiritual discipline. God wants us to pray so that we can have fellowship with him and express our concerns regarding anything that is on our mind. Until we are living with him in heaven, prayer is one of the only ways in which we can have fellowship with him here on Earth. Prayer is primarily a way for us to develop a closer relationship with God and with other individuals. When we pray, we are telling God about important issues that concern us.

It is important to remember that Jesus prayed while he was here on Earth. Jesus prayed so that he could draw closer to his own Father and to express his concerns regarding many things that were on his heart. If it was important for Jesus to pray, then I believe that we need to take the time to talk to God many times each and every day. All of us need to pray to the Composer so that we can be prepared to serve him for his honor and glory.

Confession

Psalm 66:17-19: I cried out to him with my mouth; his praise was on my tongue. If I had cherished sin in my heart, the Lord would not have listened; but God has surely listened and heard my voice in prayer.

Confessing our sins to God and to one another is a very important spiritual discipline. Every human being is going to sin but God's children possess spiritual power so that they can resist some of the temptations that are in this world. This spiritual power comes from the Holy Spirit who lives inside of them. Christians need to behave differently from individuals who do not know the Composer. The power of the Holy Spirit must make a difference in our lives or else there is not a reason for him to live inside of us.

When we sin, we should be very troubled and have a restless heart. We really need to understand that God can not tolerate sin. When we sin, we are doing something that is an anathema to him. When this happens, we must be genuinely sorry for this kind of behavior.

The Bible tells us to confess our sins unto the Lord. If we do not confess our sins unto him, God will not listen to us. This will cause our fellowship with the Composer to be broken. How can we expect God to be willing to use us if we continue to behave in ways that are contradictory to his divine plan for our lives?

The Bible tells us that everyone has sinned. However, there is nothing that anyone has ever done that God is unwilling to forgive. If we claim to be a child of God, we need to examine our hearts and confess any sins that we have ever committed. Then we need to ask the Conductor to help us to live our lives in obedience to the Composer. This is absolutely necessary if we earnestly desire to be allowed to have fellowship with him and to be able to participate in God's Cycle of Music.

Communion

Luke 22:19-20: And he took bread, gave thanks and broke it, and gave it to them, saying, "This is my body given for you; do this in remembrance of me." In the same way, after the supper he took the cup, saying, "This cup is the new covenant in my blood, which is poured out for you."

Everyone who has committed their life unto the Lord must take time to remember Christ's broken body and his shed blood on the cross by participating in the sacrament of communion with other believers. We must continue to remind ourselves over and over again about the precious sacrifice that Christ made for us when he died on the cross.

This is also a time for us to offer our gratitude unto him and to meditate on the important responsibility that we have of telling others about the incredible gift of grace that was offered to us and to everyone who will put their faith in God.

The bread also reminds me of the suffering that Christ experienced and the suffering that I must be willing to accept when I participate in God's Cycle of Music.

Summary

Isaiah 40:28-31: Do you not know? Have you not heard? The Lord is the everlasting God, the Creator of the ends of the earth. He will not grow tired or weary, and his understanding no one can fathom. He gives strength to the weary and increases the power of the weak. Even youths grow tired and weary, and young men stumble and fall; but those who hope in the Lord will renew their strength. They will soar on wings like eagles; they will run and not grow weary, they will walk and not be faint.

Every serious musician understands that they must faithfully practice all of their scales and other important études in order to be ready to face the challenges that will occur during the preparation and the performance of their music.

Spiritual disciplines are essential études that are necessary in order to prepare God's servants for their own specific performances. I pray that all of us have gained a better understanding of these spiritual disciplines and that we are ready to apply them to our own lives so that we can be prepared to serve the Composer in any way that he desires to use us.

8

Analyzing the Musical Score

Psalm 139:1-6: O Lord, you have searched me and you know me. You know when I sit and when I rise; you perceive my thoughts from afar. You discern my going out and my lying down; you are familiar with all my ways. Before a word is on my tongue you know it completely, O Lord. You hem me in—behind and before; you have laid your hand upon me. Such knowledge is too wonderful for me, too lofty for me to attain.

People have tried to determine the purpose and the meaning for their lives ever since God created Adam and Eve. Obviously this has produced an endless collection of assumptions. Unfortunately, many people are never able to find a purpose or a meaning for their life at all; regardless of how hard they search to find an answer.

I believe that there are several reasons why the purpose and the meaning for our lives are so difficult to understand. The first reason is that sin separates people from God. If we do not know God, we will never be able to comprehend our purpose and our meaning for being here. Another reason occurs because people try to find their purpose and their meaning in life by accomplishing various things in this world for their own honor and glory.

Our Maker has created us so that he can receive the honor and the glory. Seeking honor and glory for ourselves will never accomplish the purpose and the meaning for our lives that our Maker intended for us when he created the world. Some individuals assume that there has never been a specific purpose or a meaning for their lives at all. They exist from one day to another without any idea of the incredible opportunities that God has waiting for them if they would only commit their lives unto him.

From my perspective as a musician, searching for the purpose and the meaning for our lives is similar to analyzing a musical score in order to understand the various elements of music that are hidden within the composition; such as the form and the tonal center.

The passage of scripture quoted at the beginning of this chapter indicates that the Composer has examined his own Music so that he can know everything about us. If we want to know the purpose and the meaning for our own lives, we will need to spend time examining and serving him.

Many people enjoy music but they never take the time to learn about the intricate details that hold the compositions together. If we really want to understand a piece of music, it is essential to analyze everything about it. I like to begin by finding information about the composer. I also want to know why the composition was written. After that, I examine all of the details that are found within the music. Most people just "hear" music. If we really want to appreciate it, we will need to examine everything about it and "listen" to it over and over again.

One of the most important elements in music is called form. It is the way in which a composition is designed. Individual music notes are united together with other notes, over a period of time, so that a section of music can be created. The length of a section will vary according to the desires of the composer. A short piece of music may only have one section.

Composers can also combine the sections together in many different ways. Some composers will immediately repeat a section or return to that section after other sections of music have been presented. The structure of the sections is called the form. There are many different forms in music but almost all music has a designed structure.

Another important element in music is the tonal center. A music composition usually has only one tone that is more important than all of the others. This tone is called the tonal center. All of the notes in music move in many different directions for a common purpose; while maintaining their strong relationship to the one tone that holds the entire composition together.

God needs to be the tonal center in our lives. Everything that we do must be related to him. If music does not have a tonal center, every note would exist without a relationship to the rest of the music. Without form or a tonal center, music would move without any significant purpose or meaning. Without God, it would be impossible for anyone to ever grasp the purpose and the meaning for their life.

God's Cycle of Music attempts to explain the form and the tonal center that exists in his entire creation. It provides a balance and a direction for our lives. It lets us know where we have been, where were are, and where we are going.

God has a specific purpose for creating each and every one of us. Now it is my prayer that God's Cycle of Music will have a "spiritual" impact on your life so that you can have a clearer understanding of what God intends for you to do while you are living here on Earth and that you can experience the blessings of living in the presence of the Composer forever.

9

Live to Serve the Composer: Participate in God's Cycle of Music

Philippians 1:20-21: I eagerly expect and hope that I will in no way be ashamed, but will have sufficient courage so that now as always Christ will be exalted in my body, whether by life or by death. For to me, to live is Christ and to die is gain.

May Eng was an amazing pianist and a wonderful piano teacher. I met her on the second day after I moved to New Jersey. I was playing an arrangement of a hymn at Montclair State University when she knocked on my practice studio to introduce herself and invite me to a Bible study that she was starting in her home.

I only attended her Bible study two or three times. Over the next 27 years, May never mentioned this Bible study to me ever again. However, she always told her piano students and just about everyone else that she met about Jesus. She attended several different Bible studies every week for her own spiritual development. Occasionally she would even go to other countries for a few weeks at a time in order to volunteer as a short term missionary. One day May told me that she had done everything in her life that she needed to accomplish. She just wanted to go to heaven to be with God. Two weeks later, she passed away.

May's funeral was held in a large Chinese church, where they hold three services each Sunday, in order to accommodate everyone. There was enough room for hundreds of people to be seated but yet many people still had to stand when they attended her funeral.

There was an unusual spirit of celebration in the room; such as I have never experienced at a funeral in my entire life. One by one, people began to tell stories of the ways in which their lives had been changed because of May's love for God. May could play any kind of music on the piano that has ever been written, but everyone who knew her would confirm that there was only one special Composer in her life.

May always shared her love for the Composer with everyone that she would meet. When the pastor finally spoke, he said that the church that we were in began as a little Bible study that was originally held in May's home; 27 years before. Most of the original congregation was made up of May's piano students, their families and people who had heard about the Composer by knowing May. May taught her students how to play the piano but she knew that it was much more important to tell her students about the Composer.

After the people had shared their stories, and after I had time to reflect on the impact that May had on so many individuals, I realized that I needed to become a better participant in God's Cycle of Music. When I left May's funeral, I knew that May had been a faithful servant for the Lord and that I needed to work harder for the Composer. I wrote this book because I realized that I needed to find new and better ways to share my faith with others; just as May did each and every day of her life.

When we participate in God's Cycle of Music, we need to be motivated by our love for the Composer and by our love for people. I knew May for 27 years. She never mentioned her degrees in music that she received from Eastman and Julliard. She never bragged about her piano skills or her accomplishments as a piano teacher. She never mentioned the church that was formed in her living room. She never told me about the spiritual impact that she had on the lives of hundreds of individuals.

I do not recall her ever taking credit for anything that she ever accomplished for the Composer. She served him with love and devotion. May was a humble individual who always strived to know the Composer better. She met with her Agent several times a day and she faithfully practiced all of the spiritual disciplines. May also kept her eyes focused on the Conductor's baton.

May had a sincere desire to spend eternity with the Composer. At the end of her life, she was ready to go to be with him. May knew that she had fulfilled her purpose and her meaning in this world because she had made sure that other people would be able to continue to serve the Composer after she was gone. The only thing left for her to do was to leave this world so that she could live forever with the Composer in heaven.

Today May's purpose and meaning in God's Cycle of Music is still at work because she shared her life with so many of us.

There is nothing in this world that can ever provide a greater purpose and meaning for our lives than the opportunity to participate in God's Cycle of Music. God created every individual so that they could be part of this Cycle for his honor and glory. We are here to love him and to share his love with the people that we meet each and every day. This is the purpose and the meaning in life that God has intended for us all.

Postlude

Ecclesiastes 12:13: Now all has been heard; here is the conclusion of the matter: Fear God and keep his commandments, for this is the whole duty of man.

It is essential for us to understand that life passes by very quickly and that our time on Earth will soon expire. The purpose and the meaning for our lives can only be found when we participate in God's Cycle of Music. This was why we were created. The Composer has given us the opportunity to serve him if we will cry out to the Conductor and ask him to lead us to our Agent.

Many people who read this book have never experienced a personal relationship with the Composer. All of us need the Agent, Jesus Christ, in order to have a personal relationship with the Composer. If you do not know the Composer, I want to encourage you once again to ask the Conductor to lead you to Jesus.

If you do have a personal relationship with the Composer, I pray that you will use all of your talents and abilities in order to keep God's Cycle of Music spinning. Meditate on his Word and let *Soli Deo Gloria* be the purpose for everything that you do and say during each and every day of your life. May God bless you as you live your life for his honor and glory!

Romans 11:36: For from him and through him and to him are all things. To him be the glory forever! Amen.

Bibliography

Bach Edition: Complete Works (155 CD Box Set), Brilliant Classics, 2006, www.amazon.com/Bach-Complete-Works-155-Box/dp/B000HRME58U.

Delker, Dean; *The Dean of Shooting Hoops*, Dec. 13, 2006, www.deandelker.com/labels/cybernetics.html.

Farstad, Arthur L., *Journal of the Grace Evangelical Society*, Spring 1996, Vol. 9:16, "Grace in the Arts: An Evangelical Musical Genius: J.S.B.:S.D.G"; *Journal of the Grace Evangelical Society*, Dallas, TX, www.faithalone.org/journal/1996I/Farstad.html.

Garrett. G.M., Baptist Hymnal with Responsive Readings, (Philadelphia, PA, The American Baptist Publication Society, 1902).

Kavanaugh, Patrick and Barbara; *Devotions from the World of Music* (Cook Communications, 2000), April 18.

Staff: *Worship God!* http://bibletools.org//index.cfm/fuseaction/Bible.show/sVerseID/26180/eVerseID/26181/.

Biblical References

Scripture is taken from the *Holy Bible, New International Version*®. Copyright© 1973, 1978, 1984, International Bible Society. Used by permission of Zondervan. All rights reserved.

Psalm 8:3-6
Psalm 66:17-19
Psalm 95:6-7
Psalm 119:11
Psalm 139:1-6
Proverbs 27:17
Ecclesiastes 12:13
Isaiah 1:18
Isaiah 40:28-31
Matthew 16:24-27
Matthew 17:19-21
Matthew 18:19-20
Matthew 20:17-19
Matthew 27:46
Mark 12:28-31
Luke 22:19-20
John 3:16

John 14:6
Acts 1:8
Romans 3:22-24
Romans 5:1-2, 8
Romans 6:3-4
Romans 8:12-17, 28
Romans 11:36
1 Corinthians 14:33
2 Corinthians 9:6-8
Ephesians 2:8-9
Philippians 1:20-21
Philippians 2:6-8
1 Timothy 5:17-18
James 1:2-4
James 5:16
1 Peter 1:13
Revelation 4:11

Additional Verses for Further Study

1 Chronicles 16:23-25: Sing to the Lord, all the earth; proclaim his salvation day after day. Declare his glory among the nations, his marvelous deeds among all peoples. For great is the Lord and most worthy of praise; he is to be feared above all gods.

Psalm 33:11: But the plans of the Lord stand firm forever, the purposes of his heart through all generations.

Psalm 100: Shout for joy to the Lord, all the earth. Worship the Lord with gladness; come before him with joyful songs. Know that the Lord is God. It is he who made us, and we are his; we are his people, the sheep of his pasture. Enter his gates with thanksgiving and his courts with praise; give thanks to him and praise his name. For the Lord is good and his love endures forever; his faithfulness continues through all generations.

Psalm 138:8: The Lord will fulfill his purpose for me; your love, O Lord, endures forever—do not abandon the works of your hands.

Psalm 150: Praise the Lord. Praise God in his sanctuary; praise him in his mighty heavens. Praise him for his acts of power; praise him for his surpassing greatness. Praise him with the sounding of the trumpet, praise him with the harp and lyre, praise him with tambourine and dancing, praise him with the strings and flute, praise him with the clash of cymbals, praise him with resounding cymbals. Let everything that has breath praise the Lord. Praise the Lord.

Proverbs 19:21: Many are the plans in a man's heart, but it is the Lord's purpose that prevails.

Romans 8:27-29: And he who searches our hearts knows the mind of the Spirit, because the Spirit intercedes for the saints in accordance with God's will. And we know that in all things God works for the good of those who love him, who have been called according to his purpose. For those God foreknew he also predestined to be conformed to the likeness of his Son, that he might be the firstborn among many brothers.

1 Corinthians 10:31: So whether you eat or drink or whatever you do, do it all for the glory of God.

Ephesians 1:10-12: In him we were also chosen, having been predestined according to the plan of him who works out everything in conformity with the purpose of his will, in order that we, who were the first to hope in Christ, might be for the praise of his glory.

Ephesians 5:18-20: Do not get drunk on wine, which leads to debauchery. Instead, be filled with the Spirit. Speak to one another with psalms, hymns and spiritual songs. Sing and make music in your heart to the Lord, always giving thanks to God the Father for everything, in the name of our Lord Jesus Christ.

Philippians 2:12-14: Therefore, my dear friends, as you have always obeyed – not only in my presence, but now much more in my absence – continue to work out your salvation with fear and trembling, for it is God who works in you to will and to act according to his good purpose.

Colossians 3:16: Let the word of Christ dwell in you richly as you teach and admonish one another with all wisdom, and as you sing psalms, hymns and spiritual songs with gratitude in your hearts to God.

The Author

Mark Paulson grew up in Granite Falls, Minnesota and began his music studies when he was four years old. In 1977 he began taking piano lessons with Mrs. Rhoda Nelson from Clarkfield, Minnesota and ever since 1979 has been a piano teacher himself. He is a member of the Christian Performing Artists' Fellowship and an adjudicator for the National Piano Guild. A lifelong entertainer and church musician, he has taught at the Montclair Kimberley Academy and the Glen Ridge Public School. He is a graduate of Montclair State University in piano performance and Northeastern Bible College in religious arts. He is married with three children.

He has performed popular and sacred music for over 25 years in many venues and studied piano with Miss Ruth Slatum, Mrs. Rhoda Nelson, Dr. Paul Satre, Mrs. Eleanor Statmore, Dr. Ruth Rendelman and Mr. Edmund Battersby. On Sundays he plays for the worship service at The Holy Trinity Episcopal Church in West Orange, New Jersey and is also a member of The Life Christian Church in West Orange, New Jersey. There are many things that Mark likes to do but the most important thing that he will ever do in his life is to participate in God's Cycle of Music.

He can be contacted at: Mark Paulson, 70 Valley Way, West Orange, NJ 07052; www.godscycleofmusic.com, or at mark@godscycleofmusic.com and www.pianocanbefun.com or mark@pianocanbefun.com. Tel: (973) 325-9201; (973) 809-0777

Additional copies of this book may be obtained
from your bookstore
or by contacting
Hope Publishing House
P.O. Box 60008
Pasadena, CA 91116 - U.S.A.
(626) 792-6123 / (800) 326-2671
Fax (626) 792-2121
E-mail: HopePublishingHouse@gmail.com
www.hope-pub.com